SECOND COMING

SECOND COMING

Awakening the God Within

Sandra Diaz, Ph.D.

To order additional copies of this book, contact:
Xlibris
1-888-795-4274
www.Xlibris.com
Orders@Xlibris.com
707111

CONTENTS

CHAPTER 1

The Beginning of My Journey

My learning about leading a spiritual life began when I was a child. I was raised Catholic and went to Catholic school, and of course, I went to church every Sunday. I had no choice in the matter really, so every Sunday, I had to sit with my parents in this little church called Rosary Church, which was next door to my school, listening to this frightening priest, Father DeAngelis, preaching or, rather, to my ears, screaming about fire and brimstone and damnation to hell if we did not follow the commandments. Later on, as I got a little older, I heard from the parishioners that Father DeAngelis was removed from the parish as he was caught having an affair with one of the women of the faithful. It was quite scandalous, but I was mostly relieved that I would no longer have to sit there and be yelled at for sins I was not aware I had but convinced that I must have committed, as I was told week after week that I would go to hell unless I would go to confession. I had not even been confirmed and was too young to go to confession, so there was no saving my soul. The devil was coming for me. I was sure of it. I was so scared that in my child's mind, I believed that I had to become a nun since there was no other way I could possibly go to heaven at this rate. That he had been caught committing the sin of adultery brought me some relief as now I could surmise that he had no credibility whatsoever and there was still a chance that I could go to heaven without becoming a nun, which I really did not want to do as the nuns in my school were just as scary, if not scarier, as Father DeAngelis.

But interestingly, despite the fear-based thinking and preaching and the punishment that was freely and frequently doled at Catholic schools that could have left me scarred for life, as a child, I remember having dreams

1

of visiting heaven and hanging out with Our Lady, Mary. Sometimes St. Joseph would be there, but not too often. I guess he was busy. I remember seeing Christ at a distance, but I could never get close to him as he always had an entourage of children and animals following him. I remember one dream I had where I was visiting Our Lady and went to the basement for a moment. I looked through the basement window and saw Christ's feet and lots of little feet of the children he was with, and I tried to run upstairs to see him, but he was gone. I remember the feeling of frustration that I missed meeting him yet again. But at least I got to see his feet and I got to hang out with his mother.

My dreams of Mary when I was a child left quite the impression on me. By age 12, I was a full devotee and joined the Legion of Mary at my Catholic school. I only went to schools named after her. As for Christ, I was nine years old when my dad took me to see *Ben-Hur*. I remember the feeling of disappointment of never seeing Christ's face throughout the whole movie. It was so much like my dreams of never being close enough to really see his face. I do remember one scene in the movie where he was giving Ben-Hur some water to drink and Ben-Hur looked up and saw his face. Then Christ was pushed away by a Roman soldier. That one scene alone left quite an impression in the heart of a nine-year-old. I could feel the love Christ had for Ben-Hur as he was giving water to the slaves. At nine years old, I decided that Christ was very special. He was a rock star, and I hoped that maybe someday I would meet him in my dreams.

As I got older and started college, I became busy and stopped going to church on a regular basis. I started taking psychology classes, where my focus began to shift from the spiritual to science. Over time, science became the truth, and my spiritual life and connection all but went away. I was being trained to question all things that the senses could not register. Spirituality and religion were the fluffy stuff we could never prove, so I had to forget about it if I were to become a legitimate psychologist. My conversion to worshipping science and factual information was complete. I worked hard to understand the science behind the theories in clinical psychology and the art of psychotherapy. I learned all about the different forces of psychology. The Holy Family was no longer a major part of my life. I was learning to be a social scientist. Clinical psychology was a very competitive field, and I had to stay focused on getting the practicum and the internships at accredited training sites. The only time I had for God was when I prayed for help to get into those sites. It would be years later before I would truly reconnect with having a spiritual life again.

My journey back to having a spiritual life happened when I was thirty-four years old. I had a series of four vivid dreams or visions that was to forever change my life and my understanding of how healing works. I was never sure what to call them as they were qualitatively different from ordinary dreams. I had no doubt that I was completely awake in the dream state. I knew I was awake, and I had complete control over my actions. I was conscious in these dreams. I had spent years going to school, studying the art and science of psychology, but nothing I had learned in school could have prepared me for what I was about to experience.

In my first dream, I found myself in this oblong-shaped room with cherrywood on the walls and the floor. I remember the sconces on the walls. It reminded me of a ballroom, but a much smaller version. I remember seeing people dressed in white lined up against the wall. I knew that the people there were no longer living because my dad was one of them, and he had passed away about a couple of years before. I remember wondering what the heck I was doing there and how I ended up there, because clearly, I was still part of the living—unless I died and I did not know it. I remember hearing or feeling the thoughts of the people in the room even though no one had directly spoken out. They were all very concerned about their loved ones who were still living here on earth. I sensed that they were very worried because so many of the living souls were suffering, lost, and confused. It seemed to me that these folks had died more recently and were still learning to communicate with their loved ones. They were all there for a meeting with a very important person to help guide them so that they would be better able to find ways to communicate with their loved ones and get their attention so that they could help steer them in the right direction while they were still here on earth.

I remember thinking that I should stand by the door when this meeting would start since I clearly did not belong in that meeting. I remember waiting and looking around, wondering who this person that they were waiting for was. I was really curious as I sensed this was a bigwig, and I just wanted to get a peek at who this was. And then my intention was to leave the meeting and not hang around. I did not realize at that time that I was standing by the only entrance and exit into this beautiful room. I was waiting and looking around the room when I felt someone standing behind me. I turned around to see who was standing behind me, and there he was, the person they were all waiting for. It was our Lord Jesus Christ. I remember feeling shocked. I said, "It's you!" I remember feeling like the little girl in the Disney commercial feeling disappointed that she still had not seen Mickey Mouse yet. The little girl was looking on the ground with her sad and downcast eyes when, all of a sudden, a shadow with big round ears and a pear-shaped body appeared on the ground. She looked up and there he was, her favorite character, Mickey Mouse, and then she brightened up and said, "I waited my whole life to meet you!" That was exactly how I felt. It was really him. He was such an incredible presence, and it was just indescribable. Finally, after so many years of dreaming about heaven and seeing him from a distance, there he was standing in front of me, so much more than a rock star. I was surprised, but at the same time, I thought, *Why would they not have been waiting for him? Who better to guide them and show them how to connect to their loved ones still living here on earth?*

I remember looking into his deep-set eyes with daylight behind him as he entered the room. It felt like I was looking into the deep blue sea. I instantly felt this intense, all-encompassing feeling of peace and unconditional love. I ran to him and immediately embraced him as tightly as I could. I remember telling him that I did not care if this was just a dream. I was never ever letting him go. I declared that he was mine, and that was all there was to it. It was in the books. I remember him being tall with shoulder-length hair. I came up to where his heart was. He was dressed in white. Everyone there was dressed in white. I was dressed in white. I felt the fabric of his clothing and the white rope tied around his waist. There were people around him and behind him waiting to enter the room. As I stood there, holding on to him for dear life, I remember feeling the crown of my head opening up. An energy I had never felt before entered my body through my crown, slowly filling me up, going through my feet. I was wondering what this incredible energy was. I remember saying to myself as I held on to Christ while this energy filled me up that this energy must be his energy of pure love, that Christ is made of pure love. He literally filled me up with his love. I was in complete awe of his presence. Then the dream ended. I remember suddenly sitting up in bed and saying to myself, "I think I met Jesus Christ!" I wondered what had just happened. The side effect of the dream was that this feeling of pure love stayed with me for a few days. I was in complete bliss. Then, inevitably, life went on, and I had to come back to the real world. I got busy, and that feeling of pure love dissipated.

A few months later, I had the second dream. In this dream, I was standing on the shore of the Sea of Galilee. Somehow I just knew that's where I was. I had never seen pictures of it and had never travelled there, but there was no doubt in my mind that this was the location from where the disciples launched their fishing boats. I took a look around, and the landscape of one side of the sea was completely different from the other side. Across from where I was standing, I saw rolling hills, and where I was, there were jagged cliffs. A short distance away from the shore was a couple of people wearing what looked like shrouds. They were walking on water. I remember saying to myself, "Hey, I wanna do that. I wanna walk on water." I wanted to talk to these people, and so I would have had to do so anyhow if I were to reach them to talk to them. So I started walking on water. I remember how amazing it felt and thinking, *Wow, I'm actually walking on water.* The water was very cool under my feet, and I could feel the water holding me up, as if I were walking on a water bed without the rubber sheet that contained the water. It was such an incredible feeling, until thoughts of self-doubt and fear entered my mind. As soon as I started thinking that I should not have been able to walk on water, I started sinking into the water a few inches. Now I was really afraid. My feet came in contact with some plants in the water, which were cutting up my feet. I took a few more steps and felt a lot of pain as my feet were being cut open, and at that point, I decided that I could not go any farther as my feet were starting to bleed. I told myself that I needed to find my shoes to protect my feet so that I could continue to work on walking on water toward the two people in shrouds who were at the distance. I stepped back on shore and went around some shrubs or bushes, looking for my shoes. I went around some trees and found, around the corner, some sort of pond with a safety net under water. At this "training" pond, people were practicing how to walk on water before walking on the sea. I ran into one of my colleagues there, who was wearing her Gucci shoes and complaining that her shoes would be ruined in the pond. I said to her, "Come on now, Maria. After all, you are learning to walk on water. Who cares about your shoes?" Here I was looking for my own shoes. Then one of the people wondered how he would ever get to heaven if he could not even have enough faith to walk on water. The people agreed, complaining that walking on water is much harder than it looks and their chances of getting to heaven were slim to none.

I spoke out, and I vehemently disagreed. I told them I had been to heaven and that it was easy to get there as I had traveled there as a child several times and hung out mostly with Mary. I told them that I would show them. I remember feeling very excited that this was an opportunity to share with people what I had experienced. It felt lonely not to be able to talk with other people about what heaven was like, and now I could actually show them and not feel so alone. It was nightfall, and there was a full moon. It was a beautiful, starry night. The sky was lit up, and the full moon was reflecting off the sea. We stood alongside the cliff. We all held hands, and I told them to think of themselves as being as light as a feather but also being *light*. We all jumped off the side of the cliff overlooking the Sea of Galilee and started floating upward toward heaven. Once again, as soon as I had thought to myself, *You can't fly!* I was suddenly filled with self-doubt and fear. I could feel myself starting to become heavy. I was slowly floating downward toward the ground. The others, seeing what was happening to me, were then filled with fear, and they started to slowly float downward to the ground as well. We all reached the sandy beach area by the cliffs, and I remember becoming frustrated and looking up toward heaven. I remember saying, "I tell you I've been there. I just have to remember how I got there. I just have to find a way." All of a sudden, a beam of green light, like a laser beam, appeared. I said to the people around me, "Look, here is the line between heaven and earth. Let me float alongside this beam toward heaven, and you all just follow me." So I did, and every time I had self-doubt and fear, I felt myself floating downward, and I had to work on emptying my mind of all self-doubt and fear and focus on the fact that I really had visited heaven and had met Christ there.

I finally reached heaven and was in a garden. In the middle of this garden was a large gray marble platform with two steps. There was a white picket fence and a trellis in the middle of this platform. The grass was very green, and there were all kinds of different-colored flowers everywhere. Behind the white picket fence was just this expanse of white light, and I knew that this light was God. As I stood before God, he said, "What can I do for you?" I was in a particularly sassy mood, and I said to God, "What can you do for me? Let me tell you what you can do for me. You are the father, after all, and I am the child, and I am filing a complaint." Out of my mouth came a litany of complaints. I complained that I did not understand what the purpose of life was. I told God that in my short time on this planet, I found that human beings were generally mean to each other and lacked morals and compassion. Then there were greed, wars, strife, hunger, pessimism, crime. I told him I was not a happy camper, and I wished I never bothered to come to earth. I went on and on until I was done with my list of complaints. The bottom line was I told God I did not really understand what we were doing here as so many people were suffering and there did not seem to be any end in sight to all the suffering in the world. God then said, "Step into the light." So I walked up the two steps and across the marble platform, went past the white picket fence, and stepped into the light. It was white, with silver and white sparkles flying everywhere. I was like a kid in some kind of wonderland, trying to catch the silver sparkles with my hand. What I remember most clearly was the energy in the light. It was the same energy that filled me up when I was in the arms of Christ. I said to myself, "Wow, God is made of the same energy too." I was being bathed in his pure love, and I was being filled up again with God's love. I felt like I was born again and that the answer to my question was love. It was all about love. It was true that love could heal all things. All my negative thoughts and emotions were being cleansed away, and as soon as I was filled up with this light again, I stepped out of the light and walked on to the gray marble platform. Then God asked me, "What else can I do for you?" I told God that I missed being with Christ and all I really wanted was to be able to give him a hug. Then, Christ walked out of the light of God's pure love. I ran toward him once again, but this time, my arms and legs were tightly wrapped around him, like a little kid, as if to make doubly sure that I could hold on to him as tightly as I could. Then a thought entered my mind, stating, *Where are my manners? After all, I am standing before God.* I felt my feet fall to the floor, and I gave Christ a proper adult hug, still never wanting to let him go. I did not want the dream to end, but inevitably, it ended and it was time to wake up. Once again, that feeling of pure love stayed with me for a few days. Life went on, I got busy, and that feeling dissipated.

A few months later, I had the third dream. In the dream, I decided that I was going up to heaven for a visit. I was floating up toward heaven and was met with a glass barrier, a glass ceiling if you will. I was annoyed by this and wondered who dared to put the glass barrier there, preventing me from reaching heaven. Deep down, I knew I had put the glass barrier there. I knew it was the manifestation of my self-doubt and fear and that these were the emotions that were creating the barrier to my reaching heaven. I was hovering in the sky, feeling a little indignant about the whole situation, looking for someone else to blame for this barrier. All of a sudden, Christ appeared alongside me and gently took my hand. He told me to make a fist with my other hand and said, "Let's go." I broke through the glass barrier, but I also had to break through seven different ceilings or levels, or seven somethings, before I reached heaven. Each level was made up of different color and pattern. They reminded me of tiles. I found it curious that I had to break through seven of these things. I did not quite know what they were supposed to represent. I shared this dream with one of my colleagues at work, and he mentioned that he was studying Buddhism and that he learned that there are seven levels of consciousness before one reaches nirvana. I had never formally studied Buddhism and was not aware of how many levels of consciousness there were and what each level was. I was just curious. I filed that knowledge in the back of my mind and did not give it much further thought. It would be years later, after I had been training at the VA medical center, that the topic of consciousness would come up.

The fourth and last dream came a few months later. It was around the anniversary of my dad's passing. I was driving home from work, and I was thinking about how his hands were always soft and warm. My dad was a jazz musician and always made sure that his hands were limber and warmed up before he performed on his saxophone. I remember talking to him and saying, "Gee, I really miss your hands." That night I had a dream that I was floating on a cloud to heaven. When I finally reached heaven, I found myself in a beautiful place, like a national park. The colors were so rich and vibrant. I finally stopped on my cloud as I had reached my destination. Across from me was another cloud with an oval-shaped-light form and hands sticking out of them. I remember I was overjoyed as I knew this was my dad. I recognized his hands. I remember saying to myself, "So this is what we really look like without a body. We are really made of light. I remember going to catechism classes and being told that we are made in the image of God. Growing up in a Catholic school, I really had no idea what that meant. It made no sense to me. Seeing my dad as a smaller version of the light gave this teaching a new meaning for me. For the first time, it started to make sense that since his light is pure love and we are essentially made of this light, so maybe what that means is that we must also be love."

After these four dreams, I started reading voraciously over the next decade or so. I searched for books of people who had seen Christ or God in visions, dreams, or visits. The question I kept asking myself was "What was that all about?" I really felt like I was there, that I was awake in my sleep, that I was conscious, that I had complete control over my body and my mind. I looked at the research on near-death experiences, consciousness, mind-body connection, and anything I could get my hands on to see if I could explain what I had experienced. I was still skeptical. I was in the field of psychology. I thought I had some idea of how the mind worked, and what I had experienced was pretty much outside the box of what I learned in my training as a psychologist. My mind being what it was needed some kind of convergent validity. I wanted know if I were just making it all up or if I really did see God, Christ, and heaven. I wanted to know if that energy I felt in two of those dreams was real. It took me a long time to really talk about what I experienced. In the end, I had to conclude that I could not have made that energy up, that I did have an experience. I had met a few native people up in Canada a few years later, and I felt safe enough to share my dreams with them as they had a much better grasp on the spiritual. One of the women said to me, "You had yourself a visit." I talked to one of my colleagues, expressing my doubt about my experience, and he asked me how I could have made up something that I had no idea even existed. It was hard to argue with that. Over time, with the books and lectures I had attended, trying to understand what I was supposed to do with the information, it changed the way I connected with people. I started to wonder about the phenomenon miracle. I looked at saints and what made them special and if they talked about pure love as a physical phenomenon. I grew up Catholic but never really did pay attention to the stories or the details. I became dissatisfied with what I was learning about therapy and how sometimes it seemed to take so long for changes to happen. I started to experiment with different techniques that I will share in later chapters. I tried all the approaches myself to understand how they work and whether the premise upon which these approaches were based held muster. I would have no credibility if I were suggesting an approach I actually never tested myself, and so it made sense to make sure I would be able to explain the steps to achieve the results.

I had to conclude that pure love in the form of compassion is the most powerful force of healing in the universe. After reading other people's experiences with Christ, I had to conclude that he has never really left us. He has been among us, visiting many different people. There have been so many stories worldwide in different countries during different eras. I started to wonder about the Second Coming and what other ways might be to understand this. I had to conclude for myself that the Second Coming perhaps had more to do with us, that it had to do with the awakening of the God within us, that we are truly made of the energy of this light, and that we can change and heal the world through compassion, accessing the light already within us.

With the encouragement of the people I have had the privilege of working with in therapy, I have written down what I have learned over the years. This is my attempt to put in one book as much of the information as I can from as many different sources as I have found. Regardless of what your spiritual beliefs are or what cultural background you come from, this book is designed to help you understand the spiritual laws of the universe that work at all times. Understanding how these spiritual laws work and how to live using these spiritual laws can help you transform your life in a positive direction. This book has been written to help you awaken the God within you, or your higher self, or to give you access to your higher power. Regardless of what you call this power, my hope is that you will do the following:

1. Understand that your essential nature is made of love and light and you are a divine being. As a result, you have in your fingertips the power to create your reality in a deliberate and conscious way.

2. Understand the levels of consciousness and how we create our reality depending on which level we choose to function in. Most of us function at the lowest level of consciousness, where limitations and scarcity are created. Learning to live from a higher level of consciousness will allow us to create a life of potential and abundance.

3. Understand how the levels of consciousness and healing are connected. Because the problem and the solution are never created at the same level, learning to move to a higher level of consciousness will help free us from the limitations we have created for ourselves.

4. Choose to live in abundance and possibility rather than scarcity and fear. Learning to live in a higher level of consciousness will allow you to have a different perception where you see potential and possibilities and can focus on positive emotions. Feeling good will guide you and allow you access to the creative power you have been born with through your connection with the Source.

5. Understand that your thoughts have a frequency, as indicated by the nature of the emotions you feel connected to your thoughts. Negative thoughts, which are connected with negative emotions, emit a lower frequency, and positive thoughts, which are positive emotions, emit a higher frequency. The thoughts you send out are brought back as experiences. If you tend to have negative experiences, it is important to understand the kinds of thoughts you tend to have and the core beliefs that underlie those thoughts. Your mind needs constant confirmation of your core beliefs, and if you hold negative core beliefs about yourself, whether you are conscious of them or not, the universe will bring back experiences to confirm those beliefs you hold about yourself. Your experiences will not change until you change your core beliefs.

6. Identify your core beliefs and let go of negative core beliefs, which keep you from peace and happiness in your life, so that you can create the kind of life you want. What you experience in your life now is a reflection of the level of consciousness you are at. Your emotions signal whether you are centered and connected with your Source or not. Negative emotions tell you that you are off-center and living in the ego level of conscious, where limitations and scarcity are created. In order to create a more positive level of reality, you will have to identify what core beliefs you have that are holding you in the place of suffering, throw them out, and find out what the essence of your true being is and live from that center. Living from the place of being is the key to creating a life of gratitude filled with wellness.

7. Reconnect with the wisdom of your heart, which is where you can connect with the Source of All That Is. Christ taught that the mind is a wonderful servant but a horrible master. You connect with the Source through your heart's chakra. You are better served when the mind is put in the place where it functions best—as the servant to the heart.

This book is written with the last chapter being a workbook so that if you wish, you can do the exercises to help you get to the core of who you are and understand how to move to a higher level of consciousness to give you the opportunity to create a different experience, a different reality, and ultimately, a different life for yourself. You can choose to live a life of abundance, joy, and fulfillment, or you can continue to live a reality of scarcity, fear, and suffering. It is ultimately a decision only each one of us can make. I hope that the information and tools in this book will give you an opportunity to reflect and perhaps help you understand that you are the creator of your reality. You have the power to create your experience by understanding the relationship between mind, body, and spirit and the relationship between heaven and earth. You have the power to change the course of your life. This knowledge belongs to all of us. My hope is that it will help you understand who you really are, how healing works, and how what you deem as miracles can be a normal part of your life to empower you to live the life you deserve.

Namaste!

CHAPTER 2

In Search of This Thing Called Love

My four dreams seem to make to it clear to me that love is very important in healing or transformation. It seems to be the key. Every time I had even the slightest fear or doubt in my thoughts, barriers presented themselves. I sank into the Sea of Galilee. I started to get weighed down and could not float up to heaven. A glass barrier appeared when I tried to make it up to heaven. Every time I was filled with the love of God or Christ, all my worries, unhappiness, whatever angst I was carrying inside me simply went away. It was as if there was no longer a place within me that this negative feeling could occupy when love was present. I started to search for books of people who had seen Christ to find out what they said about love.

I did not have any clue how to look for such a book, so one day, I walked into one of my favorite small bookstores and asked the owner what she would recommend. I figured she was the purchaser for her bookstore, so she must have some idea. She told me that there was a book that she thought at first was hokey, but after reading it, she was quite impressed by it. It was this book called *Love without End: Jesus Speaks* by Glenda Green. I went home and started reading it. I could hardly put the book down.

Glenda Green is an artist from Texas. She talked about some of her paintings being displayed at the Smithsonian, so she had some credibility in the art community. Her story was truly remarkable. She was not a particularly religious person but was chosen by Jeshua, as she calls him, to paint his portrait called *The Lamb and the Lion*. He appeared to her on November 23, 1991, and the portrait was completed on March 12, 1992. He spoke, she asked questions, he answered, and she took copious notes.

Christ talked to her about various topics ranging from love, light, the sacred heart, the universe, science, particles, God, and reality to name a few. Prior to reading her book, I had so many questions. I had questions about why some people heal and not others. Why do some people have miraculous recovery that cannot be medically explained and other people do not? Why don't the bodies of saints decay? What makes them different? How did Christ walk on water? How did he turn water into wine? Do illnesses and diseases have to exist? Is there a cure to every illness and disease? Is it possible to cure mental health issues rather than just manage the symptoms? How does healing actually happen? I hoped to find some answers in her book. I had a hunch that healing had something to do with this energy of pure love that I was blessed to experience twice in my dreams. I thought to myself that there had to be a reason for those dreams. Maybe there was more to what I learned in graduate school. What was I supposed to learn from these dreams? Without a doubt, I was on a quest, a hero's journey if you will. I was on a quest to find out what Christ meant when he said that what he can do, we can do and more. So what did Christ tell Glenda Green while he sat for a portrait in her studio, and what does that mean for us?

One of the most profound statements Christ made to Glenda was that "love is who you are." This was a theme that held together all that he taught her. At the time that I read it, I had no idea what the statement meant. That we are love was a new concept to me. I had always understood love to be an emotion, something that we are able to generate inside of us as a result of a thought or an interpretation of a behavior. It has something to do with how we form attachments. I understood it to be something separate from us, a feeling that is responsible for us falling for someone or behaving in kindness toward someone or even hurting someone else on behalf of the person we love. I never thought of love as something we are. It just did not make any sense to me. But when I was in the presence of God and Christ in the dreams, I noted that love was what they were made of. They were the energy of pure love. In the last dream, when I saw my dad, he was made of light, the same energy of pure love. I had to wonder if we really are made of light, this energy of pure love. I had to wonder if that was what the statement that we are made in the same image of God really meant, that we are essentially love in physical form.

Christ talked about love being the power that is most associated with the heart. For Christ, the heart is sacred. He talked about the sacred heart as the connection to God, the Source, and to the universe, the magnetic center of all that we are, of all that is. In the book, he described the heart not only as "magnetic" but "silent and still," "the great generator of all your life energy," or chi, or life force, as I had always called it. He stated that "whenever you empower your heart, you raise your energy level physically, mentally, emotionally and spiritually." In the heart lies "clarity, resolve, steadfastness, intent, stillness, respect, justice, kindness, and perceptions of greatness."

I find it interesting that the heart is probably the only organ in the body that poetry is written about. I have not come across poems that are focused on other organs like the liver or the pancreas. I was thinking how a poem called "Ode to My Liver" would just sound so strange. But as Glenda mentions, so many positive things have been written about the heart, along with heartaches and heartbreaks. She mentions how the heart is often understood as the center. In fact, when you look at the Chinese character for universal love, in the very center of that character is the character that represents the heart. She comments that while physicians note that the heart is stronger than it has ever been, heart disease is still the number one cause of death in the nation. I find it interesting that while Christ teaches that the heart is our connection to God and all that is, medical literatures are stating that we are experiencing problems so severe that people are dying from them. What is accounting for the imbalance? Are we so disconnected from our center that this is manifesting in the form of heart diseases?

In Glenda's book, Christ taught her about the relationship between the heart and the mind. He talked about how the mind is a wonderful servant to the heart but a horrible master. He taught that the mind functions best when it "integrates or projects from experience, or else it develops a logical matrix to serve, explain, and implement the powers of the heart and the soul." Its job is "to observe, integrate, understand, and implement reality." He explained that the mind, having no power of its own, if given the opportunity, will exploit the heart's troubles to compensate for its lack of power. He stated that beliefs and attitudes connect the heart and the mind. When the heart is burdened with negative feelings, the mind generates negative beliefs and attitudes that reflect insufficiency, insecurity, fear, or anger. The mind will find the heart's despair and use it as a basis to dominate it.

Because the heart is ruled by compassion, it will often accept responsibility for pain and distress caused by others, which often creates feelings of guilt, remorse, fear, and grief. He stated that to restore the power of the heart and be in this world and not of this world, it is important to have compassion for the troubles of the world and not to allow ourselves to be entangled with them but to remain "in the true bliss of the heart that knows only perfection." Not allowing negative feelings to permeate the sacred center, which can result in negative beliefs and attitudes, is the key to remaining in true bliss. Simply put, being the love that you are and being compassionate without being entangled with the negative beliefs and attitudes of others will keep the heart in its rightful place of master to the mind. While the heart can formulate beliefs to maintain its command, it is important to remember that the mind will also create beliefs to explain the heart's contents that the mind finds confusing in order to maintain control. When the mind creates these kinds of explanations, this will often result in dysfunctional actions and attractions.

What I came away with is an understanding that the mind, when allowed to have control, becomes dysfunctional as it is, in a sense, two dimensional and fear based. Christ taught Glenda that the mind will work overtime to compensate for that with which it is not comfortable to regain a sense of control. We all have experienced how the mind will make up explanations for events it does not understand, as the mind cannot deal with ambiguity or the unknown. It is weakest when it is in charge. Christ gave an example that we can all relate to—our relationship with money. He stated that when one's heart is focused on scarcity rather than abundance, the mind will work and overcompensate to find ways to generate money but can never truly enjoy the wealth created because paradoxically, in its quest to maintain control, the mind is actually financing and perpetuating poverty consciousness. Hence, as Christ stated in Glenda's book, "what he has earned through the mind's efforts is only compensating for lack, for the mind only solves problems of logic and balance—never problems of life. The man's poverty consciousness came about from wearing so many blinders to the abundance of life that he eventually believed in scarcity and then invested in it . . . Life is hard-wired for goodness but under the mind's control of it often appears to be just the opposite."

Simply put, a dysfunctional mind is a result of negative core beliefs. The source of the problem is never truly removed, and life is never truly lived or enjoyed. Christ taught Glenda that it would do her heart good if she would express the passions of her heart and release her fear, then she would gain a level of understanding that is much more than what she would attain through mental comprehension. After all, the heart, not the mind, is the source of higher intelligence. Perhaps so many people are suffering today from problems of scarcity, poverty, powerlessness, helplessness, hopelessness, addiction, and many other imbalances because the heart has not been restored to its rightful place of master, as so many suffer from heartaches and heartbreaks and continue to live in the fear created by the mind. Christ said that "the weary and troubled faces you see around you are the faces of those whose love is broken or denied." Love is reduced to an action or a feeling when it is no longer understood as a source power, leading to our misunderstanding of who we are and what love really is. We confuse being love with doing love, something that is separate from us rather than

15

something that we are. The heart is weakened when we choose separation from God, from the source of our power, which is the love that we are.

Christ taught Glenda three steps to practice strengthening the heart: "The first is to strengthen all of your positive emotions through daily gratitude and admiration. The second is to disempower your negative emotions daily through forgiveness. The third practice . . . is innocent perception." Christ defined *innocent perception* as perceiving without preconceptions; in other words, seeing things as they are without interpretation or judgment from the mind. Interestingly, research on the heart at the HeartMath Institute has demonstrated its central role in bringing about coherence in our mind and body. The research provided scientific evidence that the heart wields tremendous power when put in its rightful place as master.

Research by the HeartMath Institute shows that all our inner emotional states are best reflected by and affect the nature of our heart's rhythm. Negative emotional states result in an irregular heart rhythm, while positive emotional states result in coherence and balance in the body's nervous system and a harmonious heart rhythm. What they found most interesting is that the body response is dramatic when techniques such as shifts of perception and stress management are applied to increase the coherence of the heart's rhythm. What is also striking are the findings that suggest that the heart has its own functional brain, "a mind of its own" or its own "intelligence" that communicates with and influences the cranial brain through the nervous system, hormonal system, and other pathways.

Researchers at the HeartMath Institute talked about early research conducted by Walter Cannon, who mapped out the neural pathways by which the brain responds to emotions through the sympathetic (mobilizing) versus the parasympathetic (slowing down) nervous systems, responding with "fight" or "flight" versus a more relaxed response. Cannon concluded that the brain is responsible for this process. Interestingly enough, subsequent research conducted by John and Beatrice Lacey indicated that Cannon's model was incomplete as it only partially explained the physiological behavior of the nervous system. They found that the heart does not always respond as it is expected to. The heart was observed to have a brain of its own and would, more often than not, diverge from the direction of the autonomic nervous system. Research showed that the heart would send messages to the brain, which would obey them, and that the heart can inhibit or facilitate its electrical activity. Building on the work of neuroscientists and neurocardiologists, researchers at the HeartMath Institute have written in their article "The Science of the Heart: Exploring the Role of the Heart in Human Performance that "the heart is the most powerful generator of rhythmic information patterns in the human body."

In their article on the science of the heart, the researchers at the HeartMath Institute observed that the heart is "the most powerful generator of electromagnetic energy in the human body," with an electrical field that is about sixty times greater than that of the brain and a magnetic field that is at least five thousand times greater in strength than that of the brain. What is interesting is that the heart's magnetic field can be detected from a number of feet away from the body in every direction, as measured by the SQUID-based magnetometers. The heart's electromagnetic field was also found to be modulated by different emotional states and that the electromagnetic field generated by the heart transmits information that can be received by others and can affect others around us physically and emotionally. Specifically, their data showed that "one person's heart signal can affect another's brainwaves, and that heart-brain synchronization can occur between two people when they interact." Data showed that being in close proximity can result in an increase psychophysiological coherence between them. As their heart rhythms become coherent, they become increasingly sensitive to the subtle electromagnetic signals given out by others around them. This suggests that there is some kind of cardioelectromagnetic communication where information is exchanged between people and that our emotions affect the quality of this exchange. Interestingly, Christ talked about the exchange of what he called adamantine particles, which will be discussed in a later chapter, with a focus on their relationship to the heart.

Christ taught Glenda about the power of the heart, which is our higher intelligence. He stated that "when the mind serves the heart, anything is possible." However, "when the heart serves the mind there is perpetual limitation." He talked about the heart being the "sacred link to God." He described the heart as the inner sanctuary and, being in the sacred heart is experiencing "the bond between God and man." Within the heart of man lies love, and when negative thoughts disable the love that we are, we place ourselves in danger as there is nothing greater than the power of love. Only love can change our lives. Christ talked about "the Sacred Heart and seven layers of higher intelligence," which is where we can access information about how our lives are unfolding. It reminded me of my third vision where Christ was holding my hand and with gentle encouragement I had to break through the glass barrier of self-doubt and seven additional layers of what looked like boards covered with linoleum flooring made of different colors and patterns before I could reach heaven. In truth, pure love was holding my hand and cutting through my self-doubt, allowing me to reach the highest levels of my being.

Christ talked about love as "the commander in chief" and our thoughts being "the colonel giving orders to the troops in the field." For our thoughts to be effective in being the colonel who gives orders to the troops, he emphasized the importance of making sure that thoughts are expressed with simplicity. He encouraged us to "guard our thoughts and instruct them well. If you misconceive them to be the source of your life, however, you will forget your real power," for "love is the source of your life." I had to ponder what all that meant. How does being connected to the heart work? My understanding is that in order for our lives to change for the better, it is important for us to connect with the love that lies within our hearts and let that love in our hearts direct our lives. What does that mean, and how do we know we are doing that? And where do thoughts fit into this?

Christ taught Glenda that only working with thoughts to change them from negative to positive will become ineffective over time. This is because the heart, which is the source of love, has not been included in the process. He stated that to sustain the changes of positive thinking, love must be the foundation of our thoughts. As Christ put it simply, "You must put love behind your thoughts to make them work." He used an analogy of the archer, where he explained to Glenda, "Compare your love and your thoughts to an archer. If your love is the archer, then your mind is the bow and your thoughts are the arrows. Without careful direction of thoughts, you will not hit the target. Without love to pull the bowstring, your motivation will be weak or misdirected. These things are all part of your totality, yet love is the simplicity of your power. It is important to guard and direct your thoughts. Even so, do not assign them a separate power from your love, and do not think the keys to heaven can be grasped by your mind. Your mind cannot open that door. Mental activity invariably results in complexities which must then be implemented by structure. Within the hierarchies of mental structure, ideas ascend in levels of sophistication. Such complicated standards will always establish some persons or situations as superior to others. Love, on the other hand, is simple, and so is the spirit. Stay with simplicity and avoid the pitfalls of complicated living." In the end, I understood that thoughts powered by love are what miracles are about.

Glenda asked Christ about miracles, and he stated that healing requires that we place no thought on illness, unless we wish to multiply illness. He stated that to heal, we need to "love that which is well until it multiplies and overtakes that which was lacking in health." He stated that gratitude is important for that reason, for "gratitude . . . multiplies whatever you appreciate." Hence, giving with love is the key to living a life of miracles. What you give with love multiplies and expands. From one comes many when given with love, for love is the power. Christ was not talking about the love we would associate with attachment and our romantic fantasies, which is what is often portrayed in books and movies. He was talking about love as a holy power that should be revered.

Christ also talked to Glenda about the importance of living in moderation as it relates to being well. He stated that "'well-being' is the true feeling of moderation. Pursue moderation in all things . . . not only in material accumulation or in your physical comforts, but also in the food you eat, and in mental pursuits, habits, and work. As heaven comes to earth, the standard of economy will be that of moderation. It will no longer be the norm for some to hoard while others starve. Sharing will become a joy as you learn that everything you share will be multiplied and then become the basis of your own receiving." What better way to be the love that you are by being compassion in action?

Christ taught Glenda that by being in the heart, we become one with God, for God sees our spirit as the one spirit we share with him, perfect and indivisible. Glenda wondered why we have difficulty entering the heart, and Christ stated that it is because we do not see ourselves as God sees us—pure, perfect, and innocent. We see ourselves the way our minds have created us, this false image of brokenness, unworthiness, and being full of mistakes. Therefore, we stay on the edge of our hearts, looking in but never entering the sacred chamber. We have rejected the love that we are and are unable to heal, unable to forgive ourselves, unable to grow spiritually. He stated that judging, which is what the mind does when it takes the place of the heart, is what separates us from the sacred chamber. This does not mean that acts of destruction should not be stopped and offenders not dealt with. However, he stated that correction of behavior "should be applied with the intent of restoring brotherhood and not dividing or diminishing it." It is all about mutually supporting one another and living in harmony without sacrificing individuality or living in clannish conformity.

For me, judgment is the absence of innocent perception. It comprises dualistic conceptualization of the world where things are categorized as opposites. The heart Christ spoke to Glenda about was not the physical heart. He was talking about the sacred heart, "the central focus point of your very soul. It is the lens through which your soul integrates all of your earthly emotions and all of your divine awareness into a focused point of infinite possibility. This point is on the threshold of your physical existence, at a point slightly below and behind your physical heart."

Christ talked about this point being the source of power that God created within each of us. This point cannot be found in the mind. He encourages us to live in our hearts as our heart's desires will be fulfilled. He asked Glenda to locate this point in her body, and she stated that all that was required was simply being aware of its existence, and she experienced her whole framework pulsing and vibrating with energy. She described it as an empowering experience. Christ made it clear that we are not our minds and the mind will not heal us. Rather, he stated that "the answers to healing your life will be found in the inner strength of your heart."

Christ talked to Glenda about when the mind usurps the power of the heart, there will be dominance and competition, with people battling endlessly with each other and within themselves for positions. After all, the mind is about dominance and control. In the end, he taught her that only love has the power and only love heals all things. He stated that sometimes, a 1 percent change is enough to make all the difference because that's all it takes to reposition a situation that seems to be absolute and to demonstrate that it is actually relative. Only God is absolute. All else is relative. That is why Christ taught that when we judge, we become imprisoned in the deadlocks of our own minds because that which the mind sees as absolute and uses as a basis for control is actually relative. We end up being the hamster in the hamster wheel, running as fast as possible in the wheel, thinking that we are making progress when we are actually going nowhere.

Without question, learning more about the place of the heart and its connection to love and the role of the mind as the brilliant servant to the heart, as Christ put it, began to change my concept of how healing actually works. If the key to our healing lies in being the love that we are, I would have to first work on understanding what that means. I have placed my mind in the position of power, like so many of us have, and have been encouraged to perceive emotions as somehow playing second fiddle to the mind. It seemed that the idea of being emotional was somehow interpreted as somehow being unstable or weak in some way. I have always been encouraged to see the mind as stronger and the heart as weaker. Christ's teaching that the heart is actually the one that has the power, as it is connected to the Source of All That Is, had turned my world upside down. I thought to myself, *How could we have gotten this relationship between mind, heart, and spirit all wrong all these many years?*

I started to experiment with different ways to do therapy where I would be the love that I am. I had no idea exactly what that meant, as I always looked at doing love rather than being love, but for a start, I imagined how love would behave and then I would behave that way. I recalled the passage in Corinthians that I had learned in Catholic school. According to 1 Corinthians 13:4-13,

> Love is patient, love is kind and is not jealous; love does not brag and is not arrogant, does not act unbecomingly; it does not seek its own, is not provoked, does not take into account a wrong

suffered, does not rejoice in unrighteousness, but rejoices with the truth; bears all things, believes all things, hopes all things, endures all things.

Love never fails; but if there are gifts of prophecy, they will be done away; if there are tongues, they will cease; if there is knowledge, it will be done away. For we know in part and we prophesy in part; but when the perfect comes, the partial will be done away. When I was a child, I used to speak like a child, think like a child, reason like a child; when I became a man, I did away with childish things. For now we see in a mirror dimly, but then face to face; now I know in part, but then I will know fully just as I also have been fully known. But now faith, hope, love, abide these three; but the greatest of these is love.

I remember being taught that the greatest commandment of all is to love one another as Christ has loved us. If we'd live this way, it would make sense that all the other commandments would be taken care of. We would automatically treat each other the way we would want to be treated. Ego or the mind would be in place as servant, and the heart would be in place as master. I imagined that being love meant recognizing a person as also love and honoring him or her, which is not easy to do in the presence of our enemies. How does one love one's enemies? *That would be tough*, I thought.

I thought about my clients and how to apply this to therapy. I wondered how love would see my clients, and I imagined that they would be perceived without judgment. I imagined that love would see them as heaven sees them, as spiritually perfect. I would work on seeing the best in them, seeing their strengths, rather than only focusing on their deficits or their illnesses. I really had no clue what I was doing, but it made sense to start by focusing on the present, on the now, because in truth, this moment is really all that we have. I started to encourage clients to do the same and to try to look for the gifts from their pain and suffering in the past. What gift could pain and suffering possibly bring us? What could pain and suffering possibly teach us? Sometimes, through our pain and suffering, we get to learn who we are not in order to know who we really are, and we are given the opportunity to reinvent ourselves.

I started to understand that suffering can come from living in the past or living in the future. So many of my clients come for therapy because of the bad experiences they have had when they were children, and the wounds from those experience have never properly healed. They feel stuck, a kind of arrested development. It seemed to me that a traumatic past can bring sadness or depression, and this can distort one's vision of the future and result in thoughts that bring fear or anxiety. The present, on the other hand, is the only place where we really have any control. It is the only place we truly have any control over ourselves. Isn't being in control of ourselves the way to empowerment?

So many times, I have witnessed the bad behavior of people who think that the only way to build their self-esteem is to do it at the expense of other people, to step on them or to control them. The only problem with this way of being is that the people whose source of self-esteem is outside of themselves will forever be at the mercy of others who have to cooperate with them and be allowed to mistreat or abuse them so that they can maintain that self-esteem, that false sense of power. It is a place of complete vulnerability or disempowerment, and that is how despots or dictators are born, as they have to exert so much control over others to ensure that they always have a ready supply of power. The fastest way to do this is to create fear in others. However, it is an exhausting enterprise because people have to continue to be in fear for this person to be in control. Revolutions are born when people become tired of being afraid, of being under control and under attack, and they find a purpose, a reason for change. They become passionate about fighting for something. Love as such can motivate us. Love, as Christ taught over two thousand years ago, can move mountains. He taught Glenda why that was. It had to do with the theory of everything. He said that we are made of something called adamantine particle, which responds only to the energy of love. He taught that the one who loves his enemy is always the one in control, as love is the only force in existence that can command the adamantine particle, which is what everything is made of. So what does this all mean? What do love and these particles mean for us now in this life we are living? How does light and levels of consciousness fit into all this? And is it really possible to live a life of miracles if we understand how all these concepts are connected? Is that not the million-dollar question?

CHAPTER 3

In Search of the Connection between Love, Light, and the Adamantine Particles

As I continued on this journey to understand what my four dreams meant, as I had mentioned previously, I read as many books as I could on other people who had encounters with Christ, whether they were in the form of visions, dreams, actual physical encounters, or near-death experiences. I needed to know what I was supposed to do with the information in the dreams. All I knew was that I experienced twice what pure love felt like and learned that both God and Christ could not only fill people up with this energy of pure love but that they are pure love. I felt healed by this energy. I thought that maybe I was supposed to understand how love heals. Since I was already in the healing profession, maybe this information would give me a more complete understanding of how healing actually works. Glenda Green's book *Love without End* was definitely one of the books that had information on healing that I felt I needed to read. I was on a quest to learn about the miracles that Christ performed. I remember learning in catechism that he had stated that what he could do, we could do and more. I wanted to know what that meant. Did he mean that we would be able to live a life of miracles too? I wanted to know if it was even possible for us ordinary folk and how we would be able to do such a thing when it seemed that only saints were capable of such feats. In my search for answers, Glenda's book, for some reason, had a profound effect on me. Somehow I felt that I would find at least a part of the answer in her book. That was where I came across this thing called adamantine particles, which had some sort of connection to healing. I needed to understand more.

Christ spoke about adamantine particles being particles of infinity, and they are "the fundamental building blocks of physical existence—particularized energy potentials which activate, unify and give form to infinity." He described them as "irreducible, indivisible, and generic; and their very existence establishes dimension." He stated that they were the only particles in the universe that created mass. What I found most fascinating was the idea that they are "the ultimate points which manifest and give evidence of infinity, activating its potential and making possible all manifest form . . . They were the 'First Light' of creation. They are forever the light of consciousness. They provide the fuel and dynamic energy to propel thoughts into manifestation. They give flesh to spirit, as well as new life, beauty, nourishment, and healing to life. Because they are commanded by love and conform to the nature and will of spirit, Adamantine particles belong to all dimensions."

That we are made of this stuff, that they are commanded by love and provide the fuel and energy to propel thoughts into manifestation was for me an idea that had profound implications in terms of the power that we have to create whatever reality we choose. I thought about particle physics and the theory of everything and how physicists were looking for the particle that everything is made of, and here Christ was teaching Glenda about what sounded to me like that very particle. I remember learning about the double-slit experiment and how scientists found that the act of observing the particles actually impacted the behavior of the particles. It seemed to me that what the results suggested that consciousness does in fact influence matter. What I also found most interesting about what Christ was saying about adamantine particles giving rise to mass was the idea from Dr. David Bohm that mass is actually frozen light, a concept he presented in one of his lectures in 1986. In his book *Vibrational Medicine*, Dr. Richard Gerber talked about scientific evidence demonstrating that the cells of the body actually emit weak pulses of light that seem to be part of a communication system by which cells send information to each other. Not only do cells send coded information through hormones and biochemicals, cells also communicate through electrical signals through the nervous system as well as these weak light signals.

I thought about the implications of this idea that mass is frozen light, which seems to mean, in my simple understanding of particle physics, that we would have to slow down the rate at which these particles are vibrating in order to have an appearance of being solid. Perhaps that is why we are unable to see the beings of light we know as angels, as they would need to slow down their vibrations before we can see them as solid figures. In light of seeing my dad in my last vision as pure light, with his hands being the only physical part of him that I could recognize, it made sense to me that when we shed the body, our true essence is God's light and love, which created the adamantine particles. We are truly made in his image but fell into a deep sleep when we believed in our separation from him, which was nothing more than an illusion, and with this, ego was in command and our sacred heart, which is connected to his love, was essentially displaced.

Christ talked about the importance of placing the sacred heart back in the position of master as it is the sacred heart, being the center of our love, that can command the adamantine particles. It is when we are being the love that we are that we are then able to command the adamantine particles. Christ taught that "there is an ongoing exchange of these particles throughout existence. They not only comprise organic life, but also the planet, the wind, and every substance that is. Everything breathes for the whole of its duration. Inhaling and exhaling, these particles bring vital balance and connections to life. To one who is attuned, an illness is clearly revealed through irregularities in the breath of life. In the presence of love a natural rebalance occurs. This is how the laying on of hands can help restore health to another. Such is the power of healing touch or even a simple hug."

Christ taught that the best way to prove that love is not outside of us but rather we are love is to love our enemies. I thought to myself, *Are you kidding? That is to me one of the hardest things to do. It would require not having an ego.* How does one put aside one's ego and truly live from the heart? I wondered. Christ explained that because there are many shared particles between us and those who oppose us and it is love that commands these particles, they will only respond to the one who loves. Love is not an external commodity that we create. It truly is who we are and what we are made of. He taught that our command is not only limited to our opponents. Christ stated that it is even possible for us to command an approaching storm. He stated, "You would look for the motivating force of the storm, and then be the love in its presence. You can command the storm, for the adamantine particles are commanded by love. Love is the Source of everything. It is the commander and that command has been delegated to you as the child of love. This is why, in any situation, you can win by the power of love. Not by DOING LOVE. This is where you stumble. You have to BE LOVE! Love that is a burning fire at heart of any situation. You can truly quell the storm by loving the forces that comprise it . . . Behold the beauty of the storm. Behold the beauty of the forces that compose it. Love it to its very core. Find the necessity of it until you are one with it. Several things could happen, depending upon your degrees of assurance. The storm could just dissipate into thin air. Or possibly, it would turn into gentle rain. Maybe it would be redirected to another place. Or, at the very least, it would bring no harm to you. For love does not hurt love!" Glenda had asked about the woman who had touched his robe and was healed. Christ stated, "She touched my love and by that she was healed. As you touch each other, especially the loving essence of each other, you are healed. Living in isolation and living in separation can imbalance your life quickly."

This was some pretty powerful knowledge Christ imparted to Glenda. My understanding of what Christ was teaching is that love is our essence, and when we express that essence, we are actually healing those around us, as an exchange of adamantine particles between us is taking place. That love is powerful enough to command a storm. It is like being a beacon of light that is magnified because of the coherence of our hearts' rhythm and the rest of the rhythms of our body. As we are in close proximity to others around us, we help to intensify their light within as our coherent rhythm entrains their incoherent rhythms, and together we beat as one rhythm. As we are coherent and beat as one rhythm, we live in harmony with the rhythm of mother earth. I also remember learning in Catholic school that another way to think of Spirit is the Breath of Life. Illness then can be conceptualized as a disconnection from Spirit, a disconnection from the love that we are, which is the essence of our very being, our connection to All That Is. As we placed the ego in command with fear as its fuel, we ended up feeling the need to fight against everything out of fear as we went from attraction (law of magnetism) to force (the law of conservation).

The law of magnetism versus the law of conservation offered a new perspective on how to understand attraction versus force. This was something new to me. The simplest way for me to understand it was to imagine which uses more energy, when we pull versus when we push. I learned about martial arts and took aikido classes a while back. I was taught the art of using the momentum of the opponent's center of energy against him to throw him onto the ground. Using your opponent's own energy and simply guiding it where you want it to go uses much less energy than using force to push against him. Christ explained to Glenda that the law of conservation only explains physical existence, which makes up less than 1 percent of all that is. The physical, he stated, "is detectable only because of relatively stable patterns of energy and formations of structure." The mind, he stated, "feels most comfortable within structure and logical progressions"; hence, "it tends to impose artificial order." Christ stated that because of this, the mind is willing to break things, like lives, hearts, souls, relationships, or wills, to gain profit or to gain control by presenting itself as having the answer. Basically, the mind will use force to gain that sense of power outside of itself since it has no power of its own. The more fear it has, the more force it will require to gain a sense of security, albeit a false one. It made sense too that the law of conservation is about limitations and scarcity and how this perspective can very easily create anxiety in the mind, which has to gain power outside itself.

I thought about anxiety and how the mind can very easily work overtime to come up with an explanation, many times without any verification, on why someone is behaving a certain way toward us or why something we perceive as negative is happening to us. I thought about how we can easily talk ourselves into a panic attack simply by the way the mind comes up with catastrophic outcomes for things that have not happened yet. A mind that is not disciplined does not seem able to accept ambiguity. Simply not knowing why something is simply is, is not acceptable. The mind must have an explanation for why things are the way they are even if we have to make up a reason for what we are experiencing. Because the mind is fear based, left to its own devices, it is not surprising that many of us have the tendency to create worst-case scenarios, and we wonder why we suffer from anxiety on such an epidemic level. We can so easily maintain anxiety and depression just with negative thought processes. I thought about people who suffer from mental illness and addiction and how it is not uncommon for many to sabotage their own recovery just to feel some sense of control. They talk about the fear of success and how being successful can be an unfamiliar and frightening territory. Ultimately, many are comfortable with the devil they know. Because they are familiar with the pain and they know what to expect, they have become comfortable with the pain. They know how to create the pain, and they know what they need to do to stop the pain. Core beliefs of unworthiness and powerlessness support and fuel the pain, and unless they change their internal world of negative thinking, the external world will continue to reflect back those negative core beliefs and confirm it over and over. The mind needs that confirmation so that it does not think it is losing control. For me, it gives meaning to the phrase "Oh, what a tangled web we weave." It seems to me that we work so hard to create this tangled web, which is essentially a version of reality that is focused on limitations and scarcity, a reality that is easily pain filled.

Interestingly, Christ talked about there only being one reality that exists beyond any personal realities we create or believe in—"the very essence and presence of God manifested through all existence . . . There is but one spirit, the continuous and unbroken matrix of all existence." Christ described reality as a "consistent, measurable, unbiased, and uniformly predictable nature of existence which performs its ceaseless tasks without respect of special interests." He stated that our only task is to "experience, perceive and report it honestly." Glenda called this continuous and unbroken matrix of all existence the truly unified field, unified by love. Christ stated that we often fail to behold this unified field and consciously interact with it honestly because we are fixated on our personal creations and beliefs about reality rather than experiencing, perceiving, and reporting fundamental reality. Christ also taught that the vastness of fundamental reality "accommodates that many variations of it within a common whole . . . fundamental reality is not owned by the intellectually elite or privileged, nor controlled by them. It is ascertainable only by experience, observation, comparison, integration, and honesty. One's grasp of reality grows as his outreach into life increases. Reality is available to anyone who opens his eyes and ears."

That there is a fundamental reality, one that acknowledges that there is but one premise—that God is in all of creation—is a new perspective for me. My understanding is that we have choices, and when we choose separation from God, which is essentially separation from love, we allow for creation a level of reality that is fraught with pain. If we see all of creation as infused with God's love, as a manifestation of God, we would have so much more respect for it. We would have so much more respect for the Earth and all that lives on it and in it. But we see ourselves as separate from everyone and everything, so we have the tendency to give ourselves permission to destroy things around us because we are not able see our connection to them when the truth is we are all connected and part of everything and everything is a part of us; in truth, we are really destroying ourselves in the process. Given this new perspective, I started to experiment with the idea of seeing myself as being connected to my clients. I started to practice perceiving my clients as spiritually perfect. I wondered what would happen if I saw my clients the way I imagined God sees us. I wondered what would happen if I focused on their strengths and celebrated those. I wondered what would happen if I focused on solutions rather than the problems. I can only say that my clients left feeling better than when they walked into my office. They were lighter on their feet, more empowered, ready to try again. What became very clear to me was that love was indeed the most powerful force in the world. I started to read more books on the law of attraction and near-death studies, books that I was never encouraged to consider taking seriously when I attended college. They were just not evidence based. But I saw the changes in people when I changed my approach. Their lives improved what seemed like exponentially. Now I really needed to know how all this works, whether it was really possible to change our experiences by changing our thinking.

Christ stated that "when man's basic thinking changes from force to attraction, every aspect of technology will change as well." He stated to Glenda that as long as we interpret energy as force, we will continue to have difficulty with fuel and crude energy. He stated that electricity is created from resistance, which is generated by force. He stated that when our consciousness is raised at a higher level and we enter the age of magnetics, we will be able to create "harmonic, non-toxic energy." He told her that "at this point science is still focusing on scarcities, forces, and the leftover unknown—scarcity being that which is subject to control, force being that which is used to control it, and the infinite leftover being that which is not understood. Looking at infinity that way simply magnifies ignorance. But, that is about to change."

That Christ stated that our transformation from consciousness of scarcity to that of consciousness of abundance where we truly behold infinity is about to happen is exciting. To me, it could mean that people are starting to become dissatisfied with how things are and are searching for answers. Perhaps they are asking themselves if there is more to existence than what they have been led to believe, wondering if there is a greater purpose to their lives. Perhaps many people are tired of being afraid, and they are working on releasing their fears and belief in limitations, trying to create a different reality, trying to reinvent themselves. I know in my profession, where I work with people who have mental health issues and problems with addiction, the majority of them express wanting to be free of drugs and alcohol, wanting to feel good on their own rather than relying on a drug to help them, wanting to feel happiness, something many of them do not remember how it feels. So many express that they are sick and tired of being sick and tired. Perhaps they are looking to live from the heart rather than from the mind, which has imprisoned them.

Christ stated that the transition from force to magnetism "will all begin with a reverent respect for the ultimate power. When that understanding is attained and activated by a sufficient number of people, the entire paradigm of humanity will be lifted above its belief in energy as force. In the face of enough love, force loses its power to dominate consciousness. From that point on, consciousness will wake up at quantum speed, the change will be so powerful as to bring answers by the second. Until then, remember that adamantine particles respond to magnetic attraction. With regard to the human potential, the heart is your magnetic center. It is through your heart that you are attracting adamantine particles and by your love that you command them." Christ further taught that it is important to "approach reality with a humble, inquiring mind, open in heart and perception, free of judgment. If you will ask the right question, all will be revealed!" Being in the heart and not in the mind seemed to be the key to the transformation from force to magnetism. He stated that the mind, being essentially electrical and structural, naturally prefers the explanations that conservation provides despite all its restrictions. It is no different for instruments of computing, experimentation, and data collection. Christ stated that "all of them have a natural preference for electrical priority and polarity."

I wondered about the idea of this transformation from force to magnetism, from scarcity to abundance, being activated by having a sufficient number of people. I wondered if this was the idea of critical mass where only 1 percent is needed for the rest of the population to shift to the new behavior. I thought about the hundredth-monkey phenomenon. The 1 percent would mean that roughly seven million people with the new level of consciousness would be needed, seven million people living from the sacred heart, seven million people to help bring the experience of heaven on earth. That would be about the size of a large city. Can you imagine people living this way, practicing the principles or what Christ called dimensions of understanding, which include "unity, love, life, respect, honesty, justice and kindness"? The thought of the possibility of humankind living from the heart is truly exciting.

He described that "the heart is magnetic, silent, and still." He used the example of the Etch a Sketch, describing our love as the pen that glides according to how we turn the knobs, our heart as the magnet on the pen that attracts the iron filaments. He taught that by simply being the love that we are, the adamantine particles will respond to that and line up the patterns and manifestations that are a reflection of that love. The greater our love, the greater the influence we have. He stated that the adamantine particles will adjust to the quality of our love. He made a distinction between formative magnetism and derivative magnetism, the former generating electrical potential and the latter generating electrical polarity. He described formative magnetism as an attractor field where "synchronous and holographic integrations are made without electrical polarity or resistance." Derivative magnetism, however, is "complementary to electrical energy, as it holds in place the basic formations of existence.

I wonder how we would know if we were living from the level of formative magnetism or derivative magnetism. I recall reading the works of inspirational speakers like Dr. Wayne Dyer, Dr. David R. Hawkins, Louise Hay, Esther and Jerry Hicks, and Eckhart Tolle to name a few. They all talked about the relationship between thoughts and emotions and how the attractor field does not simply respond to our thoughts. The quality of our emotions reflects the level of consciousness we are at. Esther and Jerry Hicks talked about our emotional guidance scale, which is essentially the entire range of our emotional functioning ranging from negative to positive emotions, with joy, knowledge, empowerment, freedom, love, and appreciation being on the positive end of the scale and fear, grief, depression, despair, and powerless being on the negative end of that scale. Dr. Hawkins talked about each emotional state having a level of frequency with compassion or pure love, without a doubt, being at the highest level of consciousness and vibrating at the fastest rate with the highest frequency.

I could only imagine the power that pure love has to bring our thoughts, which are positively charged with it, into manifestation as it involves formative magnetism, where there is no resistance. Christ explained that "love is always first and foremost because love calls everything into assembly. Love ignites union. Love unites particles and formulates relationships. The physical agent is magnetism. That power applied to physical existence is compression." He further explained that "compression is the power of simplification applied to complex potential. The results are both commanding and instantaneous." I understood this experience of compression to be a moment of clarity where, as Glenda said, it "simply means to make 'less of more.'" In my attempt to understand the relationship between the concepts of compression and expansion in terms of thoughts and emotions, I conceptualized the experience of compression as having a moment of clarity where we are able to power a thought with a positive emotion, like love, where there is no resistance while the experience of expansion is releasing the energy of that thought and allowing it to manifest into a physical form.

Christ stated that "the primal power of love has within it a function of 'self-awareness,' 'self-acknowledgment,' and 'self-dialogue'. This is true regardless of whether you are referring to love as beings or as energy. You might call it the 'I AM' force. Through internalized communion, the whole becomes aware of its variable possibilities. Differences of potential are established and activation of them begins. Simultaneously, there is a holding and a releasing that isolates the presence of a constant center existing neutrally toward the activating variables. This field can be seen to functionally operate as the 'zero point' for compressing and expanding energy." Christ ultimately taught that "magnetism is native to primal energy. Since you are part of that energy, you do not have to generate or manipulate it mechanically. What you have to do is stabilize your connection with it through self-awareness and acknowledgment." As Glenda simply put it, love then is the only basis for our self-awareness. My understanding then is that God, the great I AM force, is love. I wonder, given that love has no resistance or limits, whether love can will thoughts into manifestation through formative magnetism. I wondered about the idea of stabilizing our connection to formative magnetism through self-awareness and acknowledgment. What does that experience feel like? Had I ever had that experience?

I had an experience when I was fourteen years old. I was again having one of those lucid dreams where I was awake in the dream. I had complete control over my body. I could will myself to move wherever I wanted to go in the dream. I remember walking around the neighborhood and noticing numbers on doors and in different places. I remember waking up in an altered state, as if I were in a zone where there is no sense of space and time but rather a sense of knowing. After I woke up, I remember taking a paper and pen, and I started to do something with the numbers I had seen in the dream. I was multiplying, dividing, adding, and subtracting. Somehow I knew what to do with those numbers. I came up with four final numbers after doing all those calculations. I had known without a doubt that those four numbers were going to be in the lottery the next day. I needed six numbers, so I just guessed the last two numbers. I was underage, so I asked my dad to buy the ticket with these six numbers. Sure enough, the next day, the four numbers I had come up with after doing all the calculations came out in the lottery. I won $150, which was plenty of money for a fourteen-year-old. My dad was just baffled as this was actually the very first time I had played the lottery. I never told my dad how that happened. I just kept it to myself.

I never had this kind of experience again. Years later, when I reflected back on my experiences, I found it interesting how I had to manipulate the numbers I saw in the dream. I was not given the winning numbers directly, and I was given the knowledge on what to do only to come up with four numbers. I surmised that winning the lottery really was not the important part of my experience; rather, it was remembering the feeling of what it was like when I was in the zone. It was an experience of knowing. I remember the clarity with which I had that knowing. I had absolutely no doubt about what to do with the numbers in my dream. It was if I were being guided. I recall athletes talking about being in the zone when they were performing at their best. Was this the zero point? I wonder. Reading about what Christ taught Glenda about the zero point, I understood with complete clarity what he was referring to.

Christ also stated, "Since man is dealing with energy defined by the principles of conservation, he understands it only as a scarcity. This is reinforced by the fact that the primary source of energy he can perceive and understand is solar supply. This supply is suffused through the whole planetary system and works its way up through all the patterns of life. Because there is limitation and dependency within this system, there is also competition. Thus the strong, the aggressive and the highly conservative forces dominate. As long as man's primary supply of energy is subject to such scarcity, there will be no system of social democracy that can last long upon the Earth. It is imperative that man hang his viewpoint and look toward physical infinity and the ultimate Source of reality if he would bring forth a brotherhood of peace and prosperity upon the earth. Within this change of viewpoint he will find both the physical and the spiritual answers for which he has been looking." As I read this, I thought how wonderful it would be to be able to bring about this transformation as it would mean creating heaven on earth.

I wondered how this was related to the seven levels of consciousness I had seen in my vision. I wondered if the law of conservation operates at the lower levels of consciousness, where the "ego mind" is most active and sees only limitations and scarcity. Christ talked about the largest structure being the unified field of conservational energy, which is made of a fixed quantum of energy, and structures in that field are exact and finite. This seemed to me to be the level of secondary magnetism. He stated that at this level, "magnetism is electrically generated within the conservation field. Moreover, for any specified amount of magnetic attraction, an equal amount of charged particles is required. Therefore within this construction, there is no direct access to magnetic potential as a source of energy. The answers to primary magnetism will not be found in this limited structure. Electromagnetism occurs within the conservational field, but there is a higher function of magnetism that supersedes those polarized arrangement and its pure energy." He talked about what seemed to be a level of primary magnetism, which is activated by alignments of infinity and powered by love. Here at this level roams the free and infinite field of adamantine particles, which is the source of the greater supply of energy, where unlimited current and future compression are available.

Thinking about my dream about the seven levels of consciousness that I had to break through physically in order to reach the level that was heaven or the state called nirvana, I attempted to figure out how the seven levels of consciousness are related to this knowledge of adamantine particles Christ talked about. The truth of the matter is, I had not thought about that dream until very recently and wondered if there was a connection between being able to connect with the Source of All That Is and the power to manifest our visions through being love, creating compression, and releasing that compression through expansion as our visions become reality. I wanted to know how we reach the higher levels of consciousness. I looked for what tradition focused on these levels of consciousness and came across transcendental meditation, which is the most scientifically studied form of meditation worldwide. Transcendental meditation was taught to the people in the United States by Maharishi Mahesh Yogi, a Vedic scholar and scientist of consciousness (Pearson 2013). I needed to know what this was all about, so I signed up to be trained.

To my surprise, it was a relatively easy process to do. The teachers taught that the mind, when allowed to become quiet, has a natural tendency to reach for a state of positive well-being, specifically a state of transcendence. This was not what I had expected as I had always thought that the mind was geared toward chaos rather than a state of inner silence and peace. I learned that deep within each of us is a deep reservoir of pure consciousness, what Maharishi called the inner reality of life, the field of unity. This reminded me of what Christ called the one reality that exists beyond any personal realities we create or believe in, "the very essence and presence of God manifested through all existence . . . one spirit, the continuous and unbroken matrix of all existence." The goal of transcendental meditation is to allow us to reach or *transcend* to the highest level of consciousness, where the state of bliss is experienced (Pearson 2013).

I learned from transcendental meditation that the first three levels include waking, deep sleep, and dreaming, with which we are familiar. The fourth, fifth, sixth, and seventh levels include transcendental consciousness, cosmic consciousness, God consciousness, and unity consciousness. At the level of transcendental consciousness, we experience deep restfulness. The total brain is awake, its functioning being integrated and coherent. Our attention becomes settled inward, and we experience our innermost self as unbounded pure awareness. At the level of cosmic consciousness, with a fully expanded consciousness, we are open to the unified field. At the level of God consciousness, we experience a refinement of our perceptual abilities, where we are able to perceive the full range of God's creation and have a direct experience of the Creator. At the final level of unity consciousness, we are able to experience the innermost essence of all things, the underlying oneness of all creation. We are no longer separate from anything. We are able to live a totally awakened and integrated life where we can achieve anything (Pearson 2013).

Christ had spoken to Glenda about how being the love that we are allows us to achieve anything. It made sense to me that if that is so, then the highest level of consciousness, unity consciousness, must be where we are able to experience the complete essence of pure love. At that level, there is no resistance to manifesting our heart's desires. I wondered if the first three levels of consciousness—waking, deep sleep, and dreaming—is where the ego mind would attempt to assert its control, along with the negative emotions such as depression, anger, and fear. At the first three levels of consciousness, where the ego mind would be the most active and in charge,

I imagine that there is most likely more resistance to manifesting our heart's desires but no resistance to manifesting the mind's fears.

As I thought more about the different pieces of the puzzle to living a fulfilled and joyous life and how these different perspectives all fit together, it started to make sense to me how important being aware of our entire range of emotion is. It is important to feel all our emotions, both positive and negative, because that awareness provides us with feedback about what level of consciousness we are reflecting at that moment in time. It made sense to me that our perception of command over our lives increases as we move up the levels of consciousness. As we feel better, we feel more at peace. We move from the level of fear to the level of compassion and bliss, from the level of force to the level of magnetism, from the level of resistance to the level of nonresistance, from the level of doing to the level of being, from the level of incoherence to the level of coherence. The mind functions from the level of servant. The heart functions from the level of master. Mind, body, and spirit are aligned. I learned from all this reading that the level of consciousness we are at creates our experience through the intentions we hold. Since love calls everything into assembly and commands the adamantine particles, which create mass, we have the power to bring into manifestation what our hearts desire. We are in a position of true empowerment. Isn't this what many of us look for?

CHAPTER 4

Being in a Position of True Empowerment

The principles of living a blessed and successful life that Christ taught Glenda are, in reality, quite simple. He taught Glenda that the purpose of life is to further God's creation in this dimension. He said, "You are here to learn the process through which sacred transformation occurs in all times and places. The raw material of Planet Earth is fertile ground for demonstrating to the children of God an eternal truth: as the internal is fulfilled, the external is brought into alignment and manifestation. Likewise, as the external is created according to the will of God, the internal reclaims its original perfection. You were created in the likeness of God to extend that creative power into all the dimensions in which you dwell, seek, and create. Where you are is where your work unfolds. You are where you are meant to be." This truly does speak to what I have read about the law of attraction, that it is the internal that is reflected in the external, that it is the internal world of our thoughts and the emotional charge around our thoughts that are manifested in the external, physical world. This principle reminds us that we need to not only choose our thoughts carefully but also be mindful of the emotional charge we have around those thoughts. The emotions we feel tell us at what frequency our thoughts are resonating and the level of consciousness that is being reflected so that, for example, thoughts charged with anger and resentment resonate with levels of consciousness where the ego mind is the most active and is in charge. When we are angry, we tend to attract people, places, and things that resonate with the energy of anger.

Becoming entangled with these people, places, and things feeds the anger and leaves us with the perception that we are stuck or trapped.

Glenda learned from Christ that the way to return to a sense of peace, harmony, and balance is simply to return to the bliss of who we really are, which can be done without dependence on external conditions to make it so. It is as simple as a slight shift in perception and listening with our hearts. He reminded her, "In the eyes of God, who knows nothing of sin, you are nothing less than perfect. Which is why the very act of sin separates you from your Source. In the purity of your heart you are one with your Creator." That being so, Glenda asked why it is that we do enter our heart more easily, and Christ answered, "Because you do not see yourself as pure, perfect, and innocent. Until you see yourself in that way, you will not enter the Sacred Chamber of the heart. As long as you try to carry all of your unworthiness and mistakes with you, you will stay on the threshold of your heart and not enter." He also taught that "being in the heart is prayer." Then and only then are all prayers answered for we are in the sacred chamber, in the presence of God, and "one with your Father" who sees nothing but perfection in us. He stated that "in that oneness your Source knows everything you need and beholds no imperfection. When you enter the Sacred Heart, you are restored in your life and you are made whole again." He stated, "How can this happen to you and the face of God not be revealed?" He talked about innocent perception and stated that by practicing this, "you can be at peace with your life and see the beauty of what is before you." When I think about the many people I have had the privilege of working with in therapy, it never fails that so many struggle with seeing themselves as whole. More often than not, it seems to me that so many of us are our own worst critics and judge ourselves the harshest. So many of my clients can easily come up with their imperfections they see in themselves and have such a difficult time coming up with their strengths. As Christ says, it is judgment that separates us from our Source. We believe what our minds tell us about who we perceive ourselves to be, and we shut out the wisdom of our hearts, which tell us who we really are—love and light. He reminds that it is when we place the heart in the position of master and the mind as servant that wholeness is restored.

Christ stated, "It is not the mind's province to create reality, but rather to observe, integrate, understand, and implement reality. It is the province of the heart to accept reality. The pure heart will accept unconditionally. Although the Mind strives to understand, it will invent what it cannot understand—or still worse, it will judge. This is a dangerous phenomenon, for the mind will invent realities that lead you away from who you are and the true purposes of your life. When you surrender to the fact that existence does not require invention—that it simply is—you will be on the threshold of actually looking into the face of God. Judgment will separate you from this sacred space. Judgment is actually the only sin of which a pure and perfect child of God is capable. Judgment was the original sin, and continual pursuit of it will keep you from the presence of your Creator."

How often do we find ourselves making up reasons for things we do not understand? Our minds have great difficulty tolerating ambiguity. Our minds need to have a reason to justify what is happening to us, and we will make up reasons, even outrageous ones, many times without any basis in reality, just to keep the mind comfortable. Is it not surprising then that we created most of our stressors in our minds first and then it was manifested in our external world? We could easily talk ourselves into a panic attack in a matter of minutes as we create catastrophes in our minds. I think God would agree that we essentially complicate our lives by the way we think. We have created a mess for ourselves, unable to get out of it on our own way, unable to truly live a life of well-being because we have great difficulty living a life without judging others, which keeps us away from the higher levels consciousness that connect us to our Source.

Christ told Glenda that "'well-being' is the true feeling of moderation." He taught that when "you are right with yourself, right with your fellow man, right with God, and right with the one spirit," you are being the "love that you are," and essentially you have "a right relationship with the heart." He stated, "The heart is a powerful magnetic center that generates life energy for the body and the soul and draws to you all the needs and requirements of your life. Within the Sacred Chamber of the heart you will feel the presence of your Creator and be anointed with His righteousness. From these holy communions, high principles of intelligence will be revealed to you and through them rightness will come to your life."

He talked about the seven higher principles of intelligence, which include unity, love, life, respect, honesty, justice, and kindness. Living by these principles can restore wholeness. Christ talked about each of us being an expansion point of God's infinity. I thought about what this meant and wondered if each of us then is a manifestation of God's love, each with our own unique expression of that love, different but the same in that we are made in his image, which is essentially love. Christ stated that we are part of the unlimited potential of God. He stated that "all reality, including material existence, arises from infinity, not the other way around. Infinity stands with God as a prior cause. As a child of God, you stand with infinity also. Infinity is the unlimited potential of God, which first manifested as awareness, then as love, next as spirit, finally as an infinite supply of Adamantine Particles that can be arranged with endless possibilities." It made sense to me that how we arrange these adamantine particles through manifestation in physical reality depends on how we decide to live our lives. Glenda asked Christ not just about how to live life but, more specifically, how to live a blessed life. Christ talked about his Sermon on the Mount and the Beatitudes. He stated that some of his intended meanings were lost in translation. He taught her what he actually meant when he taught those who were willing to listen the formula for living a blessed life, a life of great happiness. The principles he taught to live a blessed life, for me, was the basis for being in a place of true empowerment. They are the following:

1. Blessed are those who live in simplicity for theirs is the kingdom of heaven.
2. Blessed are those who are able to let go of that which cannot be retained for they will be healed.
3. Blessed are those who live in moderation for they shall inherit the earth.
4. Blessed are they who hunger and thirst for righteousness for they shall be filled.
5. Blessed are the merciful for they shall receive mercy.
6. Blessed are the pure in heart for they shall see God.
7. Blessed are the peacemakers for they shall be called the sons of God.
8. Blessed are those who are persecuted for righteousness's sake for theirs is the kingdom of heaven.

Blessed are those who live in simplicity for theirs is the kingdom of heaven.

Christ stated that although structure in the form of hierarchies and complexities is an important part of physical and social existence, he encouraged us not to introduce them into spiritual pursuits or life in general but to live a life of simplicity. He stated that when structure becomes too much a part of the spiritual realm, it can lead to isolation, frustration, judgment, and arrogance. I thought about the different religions and the wars that have been fought over the centuries as a result of judgment about who was right and who was wrong, who was good and who was evil. Christ encouraged us not to empower belief systems that limit how we approach God.

This made sense to me as I had always thought that we each have a very personal relationship to God. He stated, "Don't submit to the tyranny of hierarchies which require that you ascend in our spiritual life according to permission or protocol established by man." He taught Glenda that the structure and hierarchy of the human domain do not provide us access to the kingdom of heaven. He stated that there is but one spirit. It is not necessary to inundate our spiritual experiences with endless man-made rules and regulations that tell us what we need to do on behalf of the church so that St. Peter will allow us through heaven's gate. Growing up, I always wondered about confession and the need for an intercessor to speak to God on my behalf and ask that I be forgiven for my sins. It was like having an agent who knew how to better negotiate on my behalf with God for his forgiveness. None of this made sense. I was essentially taught that I could pray to God about anything on my own except when it came to asking for forgiveness of my sins. That would require a priest. In my young mind, I came to the conclusion that needing to confess to the priest gave him something important to do, I suppose.

Christ talked about keeping our spiritual pursuits simple. He reminded us, "Spirit is within you, spirit is of you, spirit is around you, spirit embraces you, and is with you always. You don't need the permission of structure to receive everything that the Spirit of God has in store for you . . . When you are simple in spirit, all will be given to you, merely for the asking. You don't need to acquire a new dimensionality before passing on to an even more elite dimensionality. Love and simplicity are the only requirements of a fulfilled spiritual life." He talked about our accepting that we are part of the one spirit. He encouraged us to simply be ourselves. He talked to Glenda about also "maintaining simplicity in your thoughts" and to "guard your thoughts and instruct them well." He stated that love, rather than our thoughts, is the source of our life. He described love as the commander in chief and thoughts as the colonel in charge of giving orders. He taught that thoughts that are not powered by love do not work. He talked about the importance of gratitude, which multiplies whatever we appreciate.

Blessed are those who are able to let go of that which cannot be retained for they will be healed.

Christ taught Glenda that love has two phases to it—attaching and letting go. While attaching tends to be the more pleasant part of loving, it is the letting go and saying good-bye that is much more difficult for us. He stated that there is a time for releasing everything, and in so doing, we are restored to wholeness. He talked about the importance of releasing and honoring that past, which allows for the creation of space for new possibilities to come.

Blessed are those who live in moderation for they shall inherit the earth.

Christ talked to Glenda about moderation being the "economy of blessing" as moderation brings balance and equilibrium. He stated, "Moderation is not an invocation of limits or conformity, but rather an invocation of the rationality that a person is more complete when in balance. What a person acquires is governed by what he or she can love. Through moderation, under the command of love, everything is provided." He cautioned that moderation is relative and not to turn it into a new standard by which to judge whether one is living in moderation or not. What is moderation for one may be insufficient or excessive for another. We will know that we are living in moderation when we have a feeling of well-being. He encouraged us to live in moderation in every aspect of our lives, from our material pursuits to our mental pursuits and even the food we eat. He stated that "as heaven comes to earth, the standard of economy will be that of moderation. It will no longer be the norm for some to hoard while others starve. Sharing will become a joy as you learn that everything you share will be multiplied and then become the basis of your own receiving." This reminds me of the Prayer of St. Francis of Assisi:

> Lord, make me an instrument of Thy peace.
> Where there is hatred, let me sow love;
> Where there is injury, pardon;
> Where there is doubt, the faith;
> Where there is despair, hope;
> Where there is darkness, light;
> And where there is sadness, joy.
> O Divine Master, grant that I may not so much
> seek to be consoled, as to console;
> To be understood, as to understand;
> To be loved as to love.
> For it is in giving that we receive;
> It is in pardoning that we are pardoned;
> And it is in dying that we are born to eternal life.
> Amen.

Christ was clear on the message about treating others the way we would want to be treated.

Blessed are they who hunger and thirst for righteousness for they shall be filled.

Glenda asked Christ what *righteousness* meant. He said that being *righteous* means being right with yourself, your fellow man, God, and the one spirit. He stated that by having the right relationship with the heart, we will naturally be the love that we are. Glenda learned that having the right relationship with our hearts involves the following principles of living: unity, love, life, respect, honesty, justice, and kindness. Christ referred to these principles as the seven passions of the sacred heart. Together they generate compassion.

Blessed are the merciful for they shall receive mercy.

Christ spoke to Glenda about the importance of forgiveness. Practicing forgiveness daily empowers the heart and tempers the mind. It frees the soul from bondage and results in our spiritual growth. Those who are merciful and forgiving will have the greatest influence in life. The mind is unable to understand forgiveness, as the tendency of the mind is to get even so that it can balance the books, so to speak.

Blessed are the pure in heart for they shall see God.

Christ stated, "In the purity of your heart, you are one with your Creator." Glenda asked why it is that we do not enter the heart more easily if being in the heart is where we connect with God. Christ stated that it is because we do not see ourselves as God sees us—pure, perfect, and innocent. He stated that because God knows nothing of sin and sees us as pure, perfect, and innocent, it is the very act of sin that keeps us separate from him. He taught that as long as we see ourselves as unworthy sinners, carrying around all our mistakes, we will never be able to enter the sacred chamber within our hearts. It is only when we are able to see ourselves with our spiritual eyes that we can see everything around us emanating God's love. Christ said, "In the sacred chamber you are one with the Father, and in that oneness your Source know everything you need, and beholds no imperfection. When you enter the sacred heart, you are restored in your life and you are made whole again. How can this happen to you and the face of God not be revealed?"

Blessed are the peacemakers for they shall be called the sons of God.

Christ talked about many ways to create peace in our lives, the most important of which is to end duality. By ending duality, he stated that we let go of viewing life as a conflict between polar opposites, a perspective that is no longer useful. He stated that recognizing we are part of one spirit is critical to becoming a peacemaker. He stated that we have a choice to focus on the limited observation of dualistic thinking or to look beyond it and have a more expanded perception of reality. He gave Glenda the example of our concepts of dark and light. The mind tends to view it as opposites when it actually involves differing degrees of light exposure. He stated that "the conceptual model of duality is a simplistic frame of reference created by the mind to satisfy its dependency upon structure and symmetry. The mind seeks to explain rather than to understand." Duality will fade away when we achieve a full scope of understanding, when we "seek to perceive wholeness in all things." I suppose, when we begin to see that we are connected with one another in one spirit, as opposed to "us versus them," we will be able to create a world where we can live in peace.

Blessed are those who are persecuted for righteousness's sake for theirs is the kingdom of heaven.

Christ talked about this blessing as the most difficult lesson to master as it involves experiencing God in all circumstances, whether we are in bliss or in suffering. He talked about the story of Job being about this blessing. He explained to Glenda that the word *persecuted* really refers to suffering and *for righteousness's sake* really means "for love's sake." He stated that "whenever you stand firmly in the midst of a hardship, holding and expressing the love that you are, you will witness illusions falling away. Through being the love that you are, you are empowered to transcend your suffering . . . love is a power that comes from within." He stated that of all the blessings, this is the greatest. It means finding the gifts hidden in experiences that cause us suffering.

In reading about Glenda's experience with Christ, the message he gave was that we do not have to live a life of suffering. The tools have already been given to us and that in using them, our lives will be transformed. It means we have to live fully in the present and live from the heart. It means understanding and accepting that we truly are capable of transcending the circumstances that cause our suffering by simply shifting our perception and becoming the love that we are. It means understanding that we came from love and we are made of love. It means placing the mind in the position of servant and the heart in the position of master. It means taking our rightful place as children of God, as behaving as such. It means living from the heart that knows that being the love that we are is the way to true happiness and a life filled with joy. The question is how we'll make that shift. What does it mean to be the love that we are? How do we place the mind in the position of servant when we have allowed it to be master for so long? These were the questions I struggled to understand. The answers not only came from prayer and meditation but also from my greatest teachers, who are the people who have trusted me to care for them, my clients. It was through their struggles that I came to understand the insurmountable strength that Spirit has. It was my work with children and youth that taught me the greatest lesson of all, that love is the most powerful force in the universe. It is because of my clients that I am able to share with you what I have learned about applying these principles that Christ taught not just to Glenda but to us all. I am truly blessed that I am able to share what I have learned with you. It is by no means the end. I am still constantly trying to find ways to make these principles clear so that we can use them and truly become the creators of our own destiny. In addition to reading what other people in the healing arts have practiced or studied, what I am sharing with you are what I have learned from my clients so far. They are the brave ones who agreed to go on this journey with me and take the risk of trying a different approach despite the fact that some of them thought I must be crazy. They were gracious enough to give me the benefit of the doubt. They were just as surprised as I was. So here we go.

CHAPTER 5

Being the Love That You Are and Living from Your Sacred Heart

In Glenda's book *The Keys of Jeshua*, Christ stated that "God is one with reality, but God is not necessarily the same as what you perceive about reality. There are many dimensions of reality, ranging from personal beliefs and experiences to the more predictable patterns of natural order. All of these dimensions are part of your life experience. In all of it, there is God. In any one picture, there is both truth and reality. What you see is what you seek . . . truth is the essence of a thing. Reality is its manifestation . . . Your experience of reality is a direct result of what you have created, of your relationship to those with whom you co-create, and ultimately your relationship to God." Reading this and thinking of all the pain and suffering of those who come to see me to ask for relief, I wondered how to change their reality so that they can experience some sense of peace.

I have learned through my spiritual experiences, through all the books and articles that I have read, and through working with my clients that the beliefs they hold about themselves and their circumstances help to create their reality. When we put our mind in charge, the mind must have confirmation of its core beliefs. What happens then is that we unconsciously place ourselves in the presence of people, places, and things that will confirm those core beliefs. When a person firmly holds the core belief that he is a loser who will never amount to anything, most likely because he has been told that since he was a child, he will inadvertently feel comfortable being around those people, places, and things that confirm he is a loser who will never amount to anything. Because he believes this so strongly, being

---

45

successful is not something he will feel comfortable with. In fact, when he does become successful, as long as he still has that core belief in place and is nurturing it, he most likely will do something to sabotage his success for the simple reason that it does not line up with his current core belief, because a loser who will never amount to anything is not supposed to enjoy success. The challenge for me was to know how to help people who feel this badly about themselves feel good enough about themselves that they are able to give themselves permission to create a different level of reality.

This was a challenge because for many of my clients, they were barely getting their basic needs met, and they were focused on just trying to survive. How will I incorporate what Christ taught and help them understand the principles so that they will be able to apply them? They were focused on what was before them, the tangible physical reality they were experiencing, just trying to get through the day. I will have to somehow take advantage of their focus on their physical reality and help them shift into a higher level of consciousness so that they will be able to get beyond the resistance created by fear, anxiety, and depression and master their circumstances.

Christ taught Glenda the importance of focusing on love to find out the true meaning of life. Christ said, "Your experience of truth is through surrender to universal law and to the power of love. Love is the force that integrates truth and reality and is common to both . . . Your first step toward knowing the truth is to understand that personal reality, physical reality, and essential truth are not separate. They are also not the same.

"In human terms, truth is the answer your soul is seeking. The answer does not lie in data, experience, beliefs, or pushing the boundaries of reality. This answer lies in the center of your being. The pursuit of truth is what requires you to rise above the issues of polarity, resistance, and depletion that are often part of physical living. When you master this problem, it will not be because all extremes have disappeared from your life, but rather because you are operating from a realization that all extremes draw their power from a common center. All centers empower the reality extending from it."

Christ was talking about the sacred heart. He was talking about love.

So the question I was left with was "Where do we start?" Glenda talked about identifying our center, our essence, our "beingness."

As part of that process, it is important to get to know the nature of our ego, our mind, the part that many of us have put in charge of creating our reality. The easiest way to start is to identify our core beliefs or the perceptions we have about ourselves. We have to be as honest as we can as it is important to experience when we are in the mind versus when we are in the heart.

Positive qualities I think I have:
—e.g., hardworking

Emotions I feel as I read what I wrote:
—happy

_____

_____

_____

_____

_____

_____

_____

_____

_____

_____

_____

_____

Negative qualities I think I have:
—e.g., loser

Emotions I feel as I read what I wrote:
—depressed

_____

_____

_____

_____

_____

_____

_____

_____

_____

_____

_____

_____

Rank both columns in terms of which labels have the strongest emotional charge for you. Do you react the strongest to the positive core belief that you are hardworking? Do you react the strongest to the negative core belief that you are a loser? Use the intensity of your emotional reaction to the label to guide how you rank each core belief.

Think about the source of these core beliefs. How far back do they go? Is this something you were told in childhood? Write down along each core belief or label or characteristic who told you this about yourself. Write down roughly what time period this was in your life—childhood, adolescence, adulthood. For example, if one of your positive core beliefs is being hardworking, write down who told you that, such as your teacher, your mother, your friend. Do the same for the negative core belief. If one of your negative core beliefs is being a loser, write down who told you that.

Next, write down if that core belief is really true of you now. If so, write down what makes it true now. Look for the evidence and write that down. For example, if one of your core beliefs is being hardworking, write down what you have done in your life that you think makes you so, such as "I was a good worker and never liked to call in sick" or "I went to night school while working full-time and taking care of the family." Do the same for the negative core belief. If one of your negative core beliefs is being a loser, write down what you have done in your life that you think makes you so, such as "I'm struggling with my addiction to drugs" or "I haven't been able to hold a job for years."

Now ask yourself which core beliefs you would like to keep and which ones you would like to change. Write down the reason why you would like to change that core belief. For example, if you want to keep the core belief of being hardworking, write down what the reasons are, such as "It helps me feel good about myself" or "I like being able to pay for my own things, and working hard in my job helps me do that." If you want to change the core belief that you are a loser, write down what the reasons are, such as "I want to feel better about myself" or "I want to have some success in my life and be okay with that." Write down whether you think it would be possible to change that core belief and rate the likelihood this could happen on a scale of 0 (most unlikely) to 10 (most likely).

For each core belief you think is possible for you to change, write down the reason you think this is so. For example, if your core belief is you are a loser and you think it is possible for you to change and be something more positive than being a loser, you may say that the reason is because you realize that you are a person with other positive qualities (as shown by the list of positive core beliefs). Talk about what you will replace that negative core belief with, such as "I am actually a very caring person because I give homeless people money when I see them." Ask yourself what emotion you feel as you read about the positive core belief you wrote about yourself. Continue this exercise with each negative core belief. As you write down the reason why you think it is possible to change and the emotions you feel as you write the positive qualities you actually have, you are essentially starting to replace the negative core belief with a positive core belief. As you tune into the positive feelings you have around your positive qualities, you are essentially becoming more centered in your heart.

Remember that Christ taught Glenda that we are essentially love and that each of us is a unique expression of God's love. What causes our separation from that love is "judgment" and the ego, the mind, which does the judging. Our goal here is to work on creating a judgment-free zone and fostering self-acceptance so that you can begin to see the expression of your unique love. It is also essential to be mindful of the language you use to talk about yourself and your experience because the language you use reflects the level of consciousness you are at. The more fear based and judgment based your language is, the more you are functioning in the ego- or mind-based levels of consciousness and the more resistance there is to creating a reality that is filled with joy. Look at all your positive core beliefs and think about the qualities or characteristics you have that are associated with those core beliefs and put them down on a sheet of paper. As you read the list, ask yourself if you can come up with a descriptor that encapsulates the essence of all those characteristics, the essence of your being. For example, a person who describes himself as "helpful, compassionate, and kind" believes that people are worth saving, people should have lives of joyfulness and just need some direction about how to create that, and people are essentially good. The essence of this person's being may be "helper."

It is important to remember that being love is being in the highest level of consciousness. Feeling negative emotions, such as depression, anger, or anxiety, on the other hand, is being in the lower levels of consciousness, which is ego or mind based. The easiest way to move up the levels of consciousness and being in your heart is (1) to feel gratitude, (2) to be in the present, and (3) to use innocent perception, where you describe rather than judge. Counting your blessings is a simple way to create a sense of gratitude and to bring yourself into the present moment. It is in the present moment that we can have a sense of control over ourselves. Living in the past or in the future takes us out of our bodies and out of the present moment. Given the connection between the mind and the body, practicing meditation such as transcendental meditation will be helpful in learning to transcend the first three levels of consciousness and experience the higher levels of consciousness.

Make a list of things you are grateful for, however small, and write down next to it the emotion that you felt as you read what you wrote. As you feel that emotion, focus on your heart. Stay in your heart.

1. I am grateful that I am alive today. (Happy)

2. I am grateful that I have another day to practice being the love that I am. (Excited)

3. _____

4. _____

5. _____

6. _____

7. _____

8. _____

9. _____

10. _____

Now think about positive experiences (people, places, things) you would like to create in your life and write them down as if they have already happened and imagine how you would feel if you had those experiences now. Be as specific as possible. The brain does not know the difference between what is real and what is imagined. It will react the same way.

1. I am grateful that I was promoted to supervisor. (Happy, relieved)

2. I am grateful that I am making enough to pay all my bills. (Overjoyed, excited)

3. _____

4. _____

5. _____

6. _____

7. _____

8. _____

9. _____

10. _____

A very important lesson that Christ taught Glenda is that a thought that is charged with love meets with no resistance to being manifested and made reality. Positive affirmations can only be sustained as long as it is powered by love. When it loses that positive charge, it becomes harder to manifest and can meet with resistance if negative emotions around the thoughts start to creep in.

The principles of creating a life of joy that Christ taught is actually not as complicated as one would think:

1. There is but one Spirit of which you are a part. God is infused in the one Spirit.
2. You are love. You carry the light of God or the Source within you. Your light is your unique expression of that love.
3. You are created as spiritually perfect in the eyes of God.
4. Your connection to God or the Source is through your heart. When you live from the heart, your life is a living prayer.
5. When the heart is the master and the mind is the servant, you will experience a life of joy.
6. There are seven levels of consciousness. The first three levels are where ego or the mind functions. Through meditation, you can transcend the first three levels of conscious.
7. Your emotions inform you about the level of consciousness you are functioning at. Negative emotions are a reflection of the levels of consciousness connected to the ego or mind, where the intensity of resistance is the strongest and the ability to manifest our positive desires is the most difficult.
8. Positive emotions are a reflection of the levels of consciousness connected to the sacred heart, where the intensity of resistance is the weakest and the ability to manifest our positive desires is the least difficult.
9. It is important to pay attention to our use of language. How we use language to describe our thoughts and the feelings that underlie those thoughts is what determines how much resistance to manifestation of our positive desires we will experience. Using language infused with judgment causes the separation from the

Source, an increase in the resistance to expressing the love that we are, and the manifestation of our positive desires.

10. Love is the most powerful force in the universe. Thoughts that are powered by love reflect that the heart is the master and results in calling into assembly the adamantine particles (which creates mass) to manifest our heart's desires.

The secret to living a life of joy is being the love that we are. While these concepts may be foreign and strange to you, in the end, it may require a leap of faith to try these techniques. Christ taught Glenda that the purpose of life is to express the love that we are and to live a life of joy. If this is what you have been looking for, perhaps this approach is worth trying, don't you think?

Namaste!

REFERENCES

Cannon, W. 1915. *Bodily Changes in Pain, Hunger, Fear and Rage: An Account of Recent Researches into the Function of Emotional Excitement.* New York: D. Appleton & Company.

Gerber, R. 2000. *A Practical Guide to Vibrational Medicine: Energy Healing and Spiritual Transformation.* Quill: HarperCollins Books.

Green, G. 2003. *The Keys of Jeshua.* Batesville: Spiritus Publishing.

Green, G. 1999. *Love without End: Jesus Speaks.* Batesville: Spiritus Publishing.

Hicks, E., and J. Hicks. 2005. *Ask and It Is Given: Learning to Manifest Your Desires.* Carlsbad: Hay House.

Lacey, J. I., and B. C. Lacey. 1978. "Two-Way Communication between the Heart and the Brain: Significance of Time within the Cardiac Cycle." *American Psychologist* (February): 99-113.

Pearson, C. 2013. *The Supreme Awakening: Experiences of Enlightenment Throughout Time and How You Can Cultivate Them.* Fairfield: Maharishi University of Management Press.

Index

55

dreaming, 4, 34
dreams, 1–4, 7–8, 12–13, 23, 32–33
drugs, 29, 48
duality, 42
Dyer, Wayne, 30

E

earth, 3–4, 6, 11, 19, 28, 30, 33, 39–41
ego, 21, 25–26, 46, 49, 51
ego mind, 33–34, 36
electromagnetism, 33
emotions, 6–7, 10, 13, 16–17, 20, 30–31,
    35–36, 47, 49–51
  negative, 10, 16, 34, 49, 51
  positive, 10, 16, 30–31, 51
empowerment, 22, 30, 35, 39
enemies, 21–22, 25
energy, 4, 6, 8–9, 13, 20, 22–24, 26,
    28–29, 31–33, 36
essence, 10, 25–27, 34, 45–46, 49
existence, 19, 22, 24–25, 27–30, 34, 37
experience, 3, 8–11, 13–14, 20–21, 27–28,
    30–32, 34–35, 43, 45–46, 49–51

F

fear, 5–7, 10–11, 14–15, 21–22, 26–27,
    29–30, 34–35, 46, 49, 53
forgiveness, 16, 40, 42

G

Galilee, 4–5, 12
Gerber, Richard, 24
God, 2, 6–9, 12–14, 16, 19–20, 23, 25,
    27–28, 31, 34, 36–43, 45, 49, 51
God consciousness, 34
Green, Glenda, 12–20, 22–23, 26, 28,
    31–32, 34, 36–43, 45–46, 49,
    51–52

H

Hawkins, David R., 30
Hay, Louise, 30
healing, 9, 12–13, 18, 20, 23–24, 26

heart, 2, 4, 10, 13–21, 25–26, 29–30,
    34–35, 37–39, 41–43, 46, 49–53
HeartMath Institute, 16–17
heaven, 1–2, 4–8, 11–12, 17–19, 21, 30,
    33, 40–41
hell, 1
help, 2–3, 9–11, 26, 29–30, 46
Hicks, Esther, 30
Hicks, Jerry, 30
hierarchies, 18, 39
hundredth-monkey phenomenon, 30

I

idea, 8, 12–13, 20, 24, 28, 30–31
illnesses, 13, 18, 21, 25–26
imbalances, 14–15, 26
imperfections, 37, 42
infinity, 24, 29, 33, 38
information, 8–9, 11, 17, 23–24
inner reality of life, 34
intelligence, 16, 38
intensity, 48, 51

J

joy, 11, 19, 30, 41, 43, 49, 51–52
judgment, 16, 19, 21, 29, 37–39, 49, 51

K

Keys of Jeshua, The, 45
kindness, 13–14, 30, 38, 41
knowledge, 7, 11, 21, 30, 32–33

L

Legion of Mary, 2
light, 5–6, 8–9, 13, 22–26, 37, 41–42, 51
limitations, 9–10, 27, 29, 32–33
Love without End: Jesus Speaks, 12, 23, 53

M

magnetism, 26, 29–31, 33, 35
manifestation, 7, 24, 30–31, 35–36, 39,
    45, 51–52
Mary (mother of Jesus), 2, 5

25113637R00042

Made in the USA
Middletown, DE
18 October 2015